M

Men are often f
important thing
They don't always clean themselves as well as they ought to.
They spend a little bit too much time watching TV.
They can be excessively competitive.
They spend a lot of time eating greasy food and sitting down and not exercising.
They are sometimes overly cautious about spending money.
Their approach to sex can be a little . . . boorish.

But is this any reason to make fun of them?

Look inside for the answer . . .

All Men Are Bastards

Joke Book II

ALL MEN ARE BASTARDS

JOKE BOOK

VOLUME II

Nan Tucket

PAN BOOKS

First published 1994 in the United States of America
by Warner Books Inc, New York (as *The Dumb Men Joke Book Volume II*)

This revised edition first published in Great Britain 1995 by
Pan Books
an imprint of Macmillan General Books
Cavaye Place London SW10 9PG
and Basingstoke

Associated companies throughout the world

ISBN 0 330 34280 X

1 3 5 7 9 8 6 4 2

A CIP catalogue record for this book is available from the British Library

Phototypeset by Intype, London
Printed and bound in Great Britain

Two women meet on the street. One asks the other about her companion.

'Well, booze doesn't agree with him and he doesn't know how to play poker.'

'That's wonderful.'

'It would be, if he didn't drink and play poker.'

☛ ☛ ☛

What is funnier than men trying to be romantic?

A man cooks for a woman when they are dating.

He says, 'I only know how to cook two things – steak and fried eggs.'

'Great,' she says. 'Which one is this?'

☛ ☛ ☛

They say not all jocks are dumb.

Right.

Did you hear about the pro football player who was so stupid that he wouldn't sign his contract unless he got Sundays off?

☛ ☛ ☛

I ran into a man at a party who told me he had a green thumb.

'Oh, do you grow flowers or vegetables?' I asked.

He looked at me like I was crazy and said, 'What are you talking about, lady? I paint houses.'

☛ ☛ ☛

Have you ever seen a man's house? They always have the most perfect lawn. Every blade of grass is exactly three feet high.

☛ ☛ ☛

What kills me about men is they act like women don't know how to handle money.

Like they do.

I was talking to a guy the other day and he told me he lost £200 on Spurs, then he lost £200 on Arsenal, and another £200 on Newcastle.

I said, 'If you have to gamble, why don't you forget the football and start gambling on something you can win at? Like horses.'

'Oh, I couldn't,' he said, 'I don't know anything about racing.'

☛ ☛ ☛

In England, a man who doesn't do anything is called a gentleman.

In America, they call him a boyfriend.

☛ ☛ ☛

They asked me if my boyfriend's family is worth any money.

'Yes,' I told them. 'His father's worth £20,000, dead or alive.'

☛ ☛ ☛

More and more women are in the workplace, but some things haven't changed. Sometimes the best way to get along with men is to let them win once in a while.

I heard a story about a woman executive who was out golfing with the boss, letting him win.

Unfortunately, she didn't fool him. On the seventh tee she hit a hole-in-one and without thinking said, 'Oops!'

☛ ☛ ☛

Did you hear about the baby born with the organs of both sexes?

It had a penis *and* a brain.

☛ ☛ ☛

A widower who had never missed his wife until she was gone went to a psychic to see if he could contact his late wife. Arrangements were made and one dark night he finds himself talking to her.

'Honey,' he says, 'is that you?'

'Yes, my husband.'

'Are you happy?'

'Yes, my husband.'

'Happier than you were with me?'

'Yes, my husband.'

'Then heaven must be an amazing place.'

'I'm not in heaven, my husband.'

☛ ☛ ☛

Cleanliness is next to godliness, but most men seem to want to wait until they're next to God to bathe.

A friend says she was in line behind a man checking into a hotel and the woman behind the desk asked the guy if he would like a room with a bath or a shower.

He says, 'What's the difference?'

'You can sit in a bath,' she explained.

☛ ☛ ☛

You can't change a man. I thought after the wedding he'd stop drinking and stop smoking.

Instead he stopped working and started dating.

What do you get when you cross a man with a pig?

Nothing. There are some things even a pig won't do.

What's a sure sign a man is planning to be unfaithful?

If he has a penis.

Did you hear about the man who became a doctor?

If he can't cure you, he touches up the X-rays.

☛ ☛ ☛

A guy walks up to a man and says, 'Do you see a cop around here?'

The man says, 'No.'

The first guy says, 'Stick 'em up.'

☛ ☛ ☛

A man walks up to a tourist and says, 'Stick 'em down.'

The tourist says, 'You mean "stick 'em up".'

The man says, 'No wonder I haven't made any money today.'

☛ ☛ ☛

A drunk man walks up to a parking meter and puts in 20p. The dial goes to 60. He looks for a minute and says, 'My God, I've lost 120 pounds!'

☛ ☛ ☛

A man walks into an antique shop and says, 'What's new?'

☛ ☛ ☛

One man sees another man at the office and says, 'What did you do to your hair? It looks like a wig.'

The other guy looks embarrassed and says, 'Well, it is a wig.'

The first guy says, 'You know, you could never tell.'

☛ ☛ ☛

I asked one man why he had a hundred and fifty books but no bookcase.

He said, 'Nobody will lend me a bookcase.'

☛ ☛ ☛

A man comes home to his wife one night and says, 'I just saw the most amazing invention that can sew buttons right on my shirts.'

'That's wonderful,' says the wife. 'What is it?'

'It's called a needle and thread.'

☛ ☛ ☛

A beggar walks up to a man and says, 'Mister, I haven't tasted food in a week.'

'Don't worry,' he tells the beggar. 'It still tastes the same.'

☛ ☛ ☛

My best friend just ran off with my husband.

I'll miss her.

☛ ☛ ☛

Did you hear about the man who saved a woman from being attacked last night?

He controlled himself.

☛ ☛ ☛

Why don't men drink coffee at work?

It keeps them awake.

☛ ☛ ☛

Why did God give men larger brains than dogs?

So they wouldn't mate with women's legs at cocktail parties.

☛ ☛ ☛

On the way home from a party, a wife said to her husband, 'Have I ever told you how handsome, sexy, and irresistible to women you are?'

The husband is very flattered. 'Why no, I don't think you have.'

'Then what the hell gave you that idea at the party?'

☛ ☛ ☛

Driving to school one day, a young daughter asks her mother what happens to cars when they get old and banged up.

'Someone sells them to your father,' comes the answer.

☛ ☛ ☛

Why do men wear loafers?

Because you need an IQ above 75 to tie shoelaces.

☛ ☛ ☛

A man finds his wife in bed with another man.

'What are you doing?' he yells.

'See,' she says to her lover, 'I told you he was stupid.'

☛ ☛ ☛

An actor was on stage one night doing a terrible version of *Hamlet*. It was so bad, the audience was booing.

Finally the actor stopped, looked at the audience, and said, 'Don't blame me, I didn't write this crap.'

☛ ☛ ☛

If they can put one man on the moon, why can't they put them all?

☛ ☛ ☛

Why did the man buy an electric lawn mower?
So he could find his way back to the house.

☛ ☛ ☛

Why did the man sell his water skis?
He couldn't find a lake on a hill.

☛ ☛ ☛

Why did they kick the man out of the airport?
He kept throwing stale bread at the plane.

☛ ☛ ☛

A wife tells her husband to go and change their son.

Two hours later he comes back with a baby girl.

☛ ☛ ☛

What's the hardest thing to teach a man?

How to operate a rubbish bin.

☛ ☛ ☛

Why did the man come home drunk, and leave his clothes on the floor?

He was in them.

☛ ☛ ☛

Why did the man want to vote for a female President?

Because they'd only have to pay her half as much.

☛ ☛ ☛

Why did the man snort Nutri-sweet?

He thought it was diet coke.

☛ ☛ ☛

What happened to the man who locked himself in his truck?

His friends had to use a coathanger to get him out.

☛ ☛ ☛

How can you tell which computer the man is using?

There's Tipp-Ex all over the screen.

☛ ☛ ☛

Did you hear about the vandal?

He spray-paints his name on chain-link fences.

☛ ☛ ☛

What's the difference between a man and a messy room?

You can clean up a messy room.

☛ ☛ ☛

What's the difference between a man and an ox?

Fifteen pounds and a can of lager.

☛ ☛ ☛

How many men does it take to mop a floor?

No one knows; they've never done it.

☛ ☛ ☛

What's bleached blonde, has huge breast implants, and lives in Sweden?

Salman Rushdie. (So he's not a bastard – I love this joke.)

☛ ☛ ☛

A woman who had recently married ran into a friend on the street one day who asked her how her marriage was going.

'Not good. He eats like a pig, he never takes a bath, and he leaves his dirty clothes all over the house.

'He makes me so sick I can barely eat.'

'Well,' says the friend, 'why don't you leave him?'

'I will,' says the first one. 'But I want to lose another 12 pounds.'

Quotes from Some Famous Bastards

YOGI BERRA

At the pizza parlour, they ask him if he wants the pizza cut into four or eight pieces.

'Four,' he says. 'I don't think I can eat eight.'

☛ ☛ ☛

'If people don't want to come out to the ball park, no one's going to stop them.'

☛ ☛ ☛

'Always go to other people's funerals, otherwise they won't come to yours.'

☛ ☛ ☛

When asked by a friend to recommend a certain restaurant, he said, 'Nobody goes there any more, it's too crowded.'

☛ ☛ ☛

'You can observe a lot just by watching.'

☛ ☛ ☛

'I really didn't say everything I said.'

SAMUEL GOLDWYN

'A verbal contract isn't worth the paper it's written on.'

☛ ☛ ☛

'Include me out!'

☛ ☛ ☛

'I don't want any "Yes" men around me. I want everybody to tell me the truth even if it costs them their jobs.'

☛ ☛ ☛

'Spare no expense to make everything as economical as possible.'

☛ ☛ ☛

'You've got to take the bitter with the sour.'

☛ ☛ ☛

'If Roosevelt were alive today, he'd turn over in his grave.'

☛ ☛ ☛

'The only thing that holds a marriage together is the husband being big enough to step back and see where the wife is wrong.'

Archie Bunker

☛ ☛ ☛

'People hate me because I am a multifaceted, talented, wealthy, internationally famous genius.'

Jerry Lewis

☛ ☛ ☛

'When I played pro football, I never set out to hurt anybody deliberately. Unless it was important, like a league game or something.'

Dick Butkus

☛ ☛ ☛

'My mother-in-law broke up my marriage. One day my wife came home early and found us in bed together.'

Lenny Bruce

☛ ☛ ☛

'A team is a team is a team. Shakespeare said that many times.'

Football coach Dan Devine

☛ ☛ ☛

'A billion here, a billion there and pretty soon you're talking about real money.'

Senator Everett Dirksen

☛ ☛ ☛

'Mediocre people deserve representation on the Supreme Court, too.'

Senator Roman Hruska

☛ ☛ ☛

I would not like to be a political leader in Russia. They never know when they're being taped.

Richard Nixon

☛ ☛ ☛

Did you hear about the six men who went on a hunting trip?

In two days they killed eight cases of Budweiser.

☛ ☛ ☛

Two men go hunting. Soon they get separated and as often happens one mistakes the other for a deer and shoots him.

After much effort he drags his friend from the woods, throws him in the 4X4, and takes him to the nearest hospital.

'Will he be all right?' the worried hunter asks the doctor.

'It's hard to say,' says the doctor. 'But it would have been better if you hadn't gutted and skinned him.'

Did you hear about the two men who went ice fishing?

They caught 200 pounds of ice, but drowned when they tried to cook it.

What's the difference between a man and Bigfoot?

One is not too smart, covered with matted hair, and smells awful. The other has big feet.

The teacher asked little Johnny if he knows his numbers.

'Yes,' he said, 'I do. My father taught me.'

'Good. What comes after three?'

'Four,' answers the boy.

'What comes after six?'

'Seven.'

'Very good,' says the teacher. 'Your dad did a good job. What comes after ten?'

'A jack,' says the kid.

Two men meet on the street. 'You look so sad,' says the first one. 'What's the matter?'

'Well, about four weeks ago, my Uncle Bob died and left me £80,000.'

'Oh, that's a shame,' says his friend. 'But the money must help.'

'That's just the beginning. Three weeks ago my grandfather died and left me £57,000. Then two weeks ago my cousin Mitzi died and left me £115,000.'

'With all that money, why are you so down in the mouth?'

'Well, so far this week, nothing.'

☛ ☛ ☛

Then there's the jigsaw puzzle for men. It only has one piece. And most of the time, it's missing.

☛ ☛ ☛

Stupid? The power went out and he was trapped on an escalator for two hours.

☛ ☛ ☛

What does a man call true love?
An erection.

☛ ☛ ☛

Why is a man like a moped?
They're both fun to ride until your friends see you with one.

☛ ☛ ☛

Why did God create men?
She forgot to put legs on snakes.

☛ ☛ ☛

What's the difference between a man and a parrot?
You can teach a parrot to say no.

☛ ☛ ☛

How can you tell when a man is happy?
Who cares.

☛ ☛ ☛

One man is reading the paper over his friend's shoulder.

'Look at that,' says one. 'There's a woman in Liverpool who's had forty-nine children.'

'I wonder why she didn't have fifty,' says the other guy.

'I don't know,' says the first one. 'Maybe she wanted a career, too.'

☛ ☛ ☛

What's the difference between marriage and a mental hospital?

At a mental hospital you have to show improvement to get out.

☛ ☛ ☛

What is six inches long, two inches wide, and makes men act like fools?
Money.

☛ ☛ ☛

A big drunk man went to the gents' at a large restaurant.
On his way back to his seat he stopped and asked a young woman if he had stepped on her foot a few minutes ago.
'Yes,' she replied rather testily, 'yes, you did.'
'Great,' he said. 'I knew my table was around here somewhere.'

☛ ☛ ☛

Did you hear about the man who was so big they couldn't find a coffin big enough for the body?

They gave him an enema and buried him in a shoe box.

☛ ☛ ☛

How can you tell if you're dating a really dumb man?

The waiter says 'Here, boy' before putting down his food.

☛ ☛ ☛

How can you tell if you're dating a really stupid man?

He tries to decide which wine goes best with beer.

☛ ☛ ☛

A doctor tells a woman she can no longer touch anything alcoholic.

So she gets a divorce.

☛ ☛ ☛

What do you call a scrum in rugby?

A dope ring.

☛ ☛ ☛

What's the one advantage of being a man?

You never miss any important phone calls because you're in the bath.

☛ ☛ ☛

What's the most effective birth control device for men?

Their manners.

What They Say About Love

'A man can sleep around, no questions asked, but if a woman makes nineteen or twenty mistakes, she's a tramp.'

Joan Rivers

☛ ☛ ☛

'Love is like bridge. If you have a good hand, you don't need a partner.'

Anonymous

☛ ☛ ☛

'Sometimes I wonder if men and women suit each other. Perhaps they should live next door and just visit now and then.'

Katharine Hepburn

☛ ☛ ☛

What's a man's martini?
An olive in a glass of beer.

☛ ☛ ☛

Then there was the man who suffered from insomnia.

He kept waking up every few days.

☛ ☛ ☛

Why are married women heavier than single women?

Single women come home, see what's in the bed, and go to bed.

Married women come home, see what's in the bed, and go to the refrigerator.

☛ ☛ ☛

A man was ordered by a local judge to take a paternity test.

'Were you the father?' asked one of his friends.

'They'll never find out,' he said. 'They took samples from my finger.'

☛ ☛ ☛

A woman was having trouble housebreaking her dog.

'Get rid of him,' said her friends.

'I can't,' she said. 'The kids love him.'

Finally she sent him to obedience school. Her friends wanted to know if it worked.

'Well, yes,' she said. 'He no longer messes all over the carpet, but now he sits in the bathroom for hours smoking cigars and reading comics.'

☛ ☛ ☛

Some scientists decided to conduct a test to see if dogs really become like their owners over time.

They placed a female mathematician's dog in a room with a pile of bones and closed the door. When they returned, the dog had arranged the bones in a way that spelled the square root of pi. Then they put in a dog that belonged to a female rocket scientist. When they came back a half hour later they found the bones spelled $E=MC^2$.

Then they brought in the dog of a male businessman. Half an hour later they opened the door. The bones were all over the room and the dog was trying to get the other two dogs to bring them to him.

☛ ☛ ☛

Men are proof of reincarnation. You can't get that thick in just one lifetime.

☛ ☛ ☛

Nobody can call him a quitter. He always gets fired.

☛ ☛ ☛

His parents signed his report card with an X, so the teacher wouldn't know that anyone who could read and write had a son like that.

He fell in love with a woman at second sight. The first time he saw her he didn't know she was rich.

He says he doesn't love her just because her father left her a fortune. He would love her no matter who left her the money.

He's hoping for a lucky stroke. Mine.

Why did they always carry a live monkey on Dan Quayle's aeroplane?
In case the Vice-President needed spare parts.

☛ ☛ ☛

Why do men bosses have such poor grammar?
Because they end every sentence with a proposition.

☛ ☛ ☛

Why don't more men leave home?
They don't know how to pack.

☛ ☛ ☛

Why don't men cook at home?

No one's invented a steak that will fit in the toaster.

☛ ☛ ☛

A woman calls her husband at home and says, 'I won the lottery! I won the lottery! Five million pounds. Whoo-ee – start packing!'

The husband can't believe it. 'That's great,' he says. 'What should I pack?'

The woman says, 'Whatever you want, just be out of the house by the time I get home.'

What Women Say About Men

'Marriage is a great institution, but I'm not ready for an institution.'

Mae West

☛ ☛ ☛

'God created man, but I could do better.'

Erma Bombeck

☛ ☛ ☛

'His mother should have thrown him away and kept the stork.'

Mae West

☛ ☛ ☛

'I have yet to hear a man ask for advice on how to combine marriage and a career.'

Gloria Steinem

☛ ☛ ☛

'A man's home may seem to be his castle on the outside; inside, it is more often his nursery.'

Clare Boothe Luce

☛ ☛ ☛

'One hell of an outlay for a very small return with most of them.'

Glenda Jackson

☛ ☛ ☛

'The more I see of men, the more I like dogs.'

Germaine de Staël

☛ ☛ ☛

'I can't mate in captivity.'

Gloria Steinem

☛ ☛ ☛

'Whatever women do they must do twice as well as men to be thought half as good. Luckily, this is not difficult.'

Charlotte Whitton

☛ ☛ ☛

'Men should think twice before making widowhood women's only path to power.'

Gloria Steinem

☛ ☛ ☛

'Can you imagine a world without men? No crime and lots of happy fat women.'

Nicole Hollander

☛ ☛ ☛

What do you get when you cross a man and a gorilla?

A really stupid gorilla.

☛ ☛ ☛

Behind every great woman is a man telling her she's ignoring him.

☛ ☛ ☛

How do we know Adam was the first man?

He thought Eve was cheating on him.

☛ ☛ ☛

What did God say after she made Eve?

'Practice makes perfect.'

☛ ☛ ☛

How did the woman know her husband was cheating on her?

He started bathing twice a week.

☛ ☛ ☛

Why do men's hearts make the best transplants?

They're never used.

☛ ☛ ☛

What's the worst thing about the glass ceiling?

They want the women to clean it.

☛ ☛ ☛

'How often do these planes crash?' the man asked a woman sitting next to him on a flight.

'Once,' she answered.

☛ ☛ ☛

A man goes to the ticket agent after a flight and says, 'I'd like to make a suggestion. Tell the pilot to stop turning on that "Fasten Your Seatbelt" sign. Every time she does, the ride gets bumpy.'

☛ ☛ ☛

A slight woman is seated next to a horrible jerk on an aeroplane. He's loud, he's stupid, he's thoughtless and arrogant. Much to her relief, he drinks too much and falls asleep. Just as they near the airport, they hit a terrible pocket of turbulence and the woman throws up all over the man. Though he deserved it, she grabs a tissue and starts to wipe the guy off. Just then he wakes up and says, 'What the hell is going on here?' Thinking quickly, she says, 'Don't be embarrassed, you'll feel better in a minute.'

☛ ☛ ☛

Once a woman told a man that they use alligators to make shoes.

He shook his head and said, 'What will they teach them to do next?'

☛ ☛ ☛

What are the three most difficult years for a man?

Nursery school.

☛ ☛ ☛

Two men are out fishing and they are having great luck. They are catching fish so fast, they have to go back early.

'This is so great,' says the first guy. 'We should mark the spot so we can come here again.'

'You're right,' says the other guy who dives over the side and paints a big X on the bottom of the boat and they head back to shore.

Just as they're about to dock, the first guy looks at the second and says, 'But what if we don't get the same boat?'

☛ ☛ ☛

How come men don't go elephant hunting?

They get too tired carrying the decoys.

☛ ☛ ☛

Two men went hunting.

They saw a sign that said 'Bear Left' so they went home.

From the Man to Woman Dictionary 1995 Edition

Romance – Lovey-dovey junk
Dating – Drinking beer and watching football without the guys
Flirting – Absolutely nothing, a figment of the imagination
Affair – Flirting
Rendezvous – A date in France
Sharing – being in the same room with a woman, but not necessarily speaking to her
Passion – a hobby. Like watching football

From the Woman to Man Dictionary 1995 Edition

Affection – Something men save for their dogs

Love – Moonlight canoe rides, watching the sunset from a dock in the marina, horseback riding in the mountains, mulled cider together in front of a cosy fire, a spur-of-the-moment trip to Paris, a long weekend in a Vermont Bed and Breakfast, yachts in the Caribbean, tasting wine together in Bordeaux

Sex – see 'Love.'

Passion – A perfume

Love Quiz

How much do you know about love? Get a Number 2 pencil and start NOW. Remember, keep your eyes on your own piece of paper and don't spend too long on any one question.

1. How can you tell when a man's in love?
   a) The smile on his face
   b) He wears cleaner clothes
   c) The skip in his walk
   d) No way to tell

2. How can you tell when a man's not in love?
   a) The smile on his face
   b) He wears cleaner clothes
   c) The skip in his walk
   d) All of the above

3. What's the single most important thing for any relationship?
   a) Lots of money
   b) Good looks
   c) What your friends think
   d) Good communication

4. How does a man say 'I love you'?
   a) I love you
   b) He remembers your birthday
   c) He orders pizza without being asked
   d) He tells you why you bought the wrong car

5. How does a woman say 'I love you'?
   a) She gives you weird things like Mace on your birthday
   b) She drives past your house a few times before parking
   c) She shows up at your house with a six-pack and says, 'Whatcha doin'?'
   d) She says, 'I love you.'

A True Story

A man comes home one Valentine's Day and hands a bunch of flowers to his wife.

'What wonderful red tulips!' she says.

'Tulips?' he says. 'I thought they were roses!'

Romantic Places

Romantic: Lover's Lane
Not Romantic: Left Only lane

☛ ☛ ☛

Romantic: Soft candlelight
Not Romantic: Torches

☛ ☛ ☛

Romantic: Niagara Falls
Not Romantic: The local bungee jump

☛ ☛ ☛

Romantic: Ballroom dancing
Not Romantic: Slam dancing

☛ ☛ ☛

Romantic: A fire in the fireplace
Not Romantic: A grease fire in the kitchen

☛ ☛ ☛

Romantic: A cruise to 'nowhere'
Not Romantic: Going nowhere

☛ ☛ ☛

Some American students are sitting under a tree at their beautiful university talking about their classes.

Says one young woman, 'I can't believe it. My calculus course has to be the hardest course in the world.'

'Get over yourself,' says her girlfriend. 'You should try my theoretical physics class.'

'You have got to be joking,' says a young man there on a football scholarship. 'You call that stuff hard? You should try *my* class. Have you ever heard of something called subtraction?

☛ ☛ ☛

Sometimes we wonder where men learn to be so selfish.

A substitute teacher reports that recently she was teaching maths to some children. She said to one boy, 'If you had five apples and I asked you for one, how many would you have left?'

The boy didn't bat an eye. 'Five,' he answered.

☛ ☛ ☛

Where's Robert Redford when you need him?

A man is playing craps at Caesar's Palace and he's winning a fortune.

'Tonight,' he says to his wife, 'you're going to sleep with the richest man in Atlantic City.'

Just then, his luck changes. Within minutes he's broke.

'So tell me,' says his wife. 'Is Donald Trump coming to our room or do I go to his?'

☛ ☛ ☛

Men love their own.

One day the manager of a brokerage firm walks past a new employee counting put and call slips. The guy does it faster than anyone he has ever seen.

'That's amazing,' says the manager. 'Where did you learn to count like that?'

'Yale,' answers the employee.

'Yale? I don't believe it. I went to Yale. What's your name?'

'Yohnson.'

☛ ☛ ☛

He is so dumb, he thinks a pole vault is in a bank in Warsaw.

☛ ☛ ☛

Finally, the perfect story on male bonding.

Two guys met in a bar and had a wonderful time. They enjoyed each other's company, but one guy travelled a lot. But he had so much fun that he finally got the other guy to agree that they should get together once a year at the very same spot.

A year later the traveller showed up and found his new friend waiting at the bar.

'When did you get here?' the man asked.

The other guy looked at him and said, 'So who left?'

☛ ☛ ☛

A woman's boss is pretty angry with her.

'Listen,' he says, 'I know we had a little thing together, but who told you that you could saunter in here any time you please?'

'My lawyer.'

☛ ☛ ☛

'Mummy, where do babies come from?'

'The stork, dear.'

'Mummy, who keeps bad people from robbing our house?'

'The police, dear.'

'Mummy, if our house was on fire, who would save us?'

'The fire brigade, dear.'

'Mummy, where does food come from?'

'Farmers, dear.'

'Mummy?'

'Yes, dear?'

'What do we need Daddy for?'

☛ ☛ ☛

He keeps a record of everything he eats.

It's called a tie.

☛ ☛ ☛

You think that's bad? He wears the ugliest clothes you can buy. A moth flew into his cupboard once and it threw up.

☛ ☛ ☛

What's the one thing that keeps most men out of university?

School.

☛ ☛ ☛

'This coffee isn't fit for a pig!' said the rude man at the café.

'No problem,' said the waitress. 'I'll get you some that is.'

☛ ☛ ☛

We try to keep him out of the kitchen.

Last time he cooked he burned the salad.

☛ ☛ ☛

The police woman asked the lady why she didn't report the robbery right away.

'I didn't know it was a robbery right away. It looked like my husband had been looking for a clean shirt.'

☛ ☛ ☛

A man and a woman go into the chemist's to pick up a prescription. While they're waiting, the man climbs on one of those old-fashioned scales some of them have. He puts in a pound and out comes a card that says, 'You are thoughtful, considerate, kindhearted, and good with children.' Very smugly, he hands the card to the woman. She reads it and says, 'It didn't get your weight right, either.'

☛ ☛ ☛

All he does is drink beer and watch TV.

It got so bad we had to let out the sofa.

☛ ☛ ☛

At least he doesn't eat between meals.

That's because there is no 'between' meals.

☛ ☛ ☛

He weighs the same now as the day we were married.

Thirty stone.

☛ ☛ ☛

They finally arrested the man for wife-beating and took him to jail.

It took a lot of persuading, but they got the wife to testify against him.

At one point, the man couldn't take it any more and he jumped up and said, 'You can't believe her, Judge, she's punch-drunk!'

☛ ☛ ☛

A man decides to go scuba diving. He buys all kinds of expensive equipment and goes on his first dive. He's down about 120 feet when he sees a guy go by in nothing but bathing trunks. He can't believe it, he's just spent all this money, and here's some guy who didn't spend a penny having just as much fun. He can't stand it. He grabs his expensive underwater message board and scribbles a note to the other guy, 'How can you dive this deep without any equipment?'

The man in the bathing trunks grabs the board and writes, 'I'm drowning, you jerk!'

☛ ☛ ☛

Two drunks are walking down the street together in a tough waterfront neighbourhood. They see a young punk siphoning petrol out of a car.

'Man,' says one drunk, 'I hope I never get that thirsty.'

☛ ☛ ☛

Dull? He's the poster boy for grey-beige.

☛ ☛ ☛

I don't know where men learn to eat. On more than one occasion I've had to explain to them what a tablecloth is. I've also had to tell them that when they hit it, it's time to stop eating.

Men Stumpers

How much expensive exercise equipment do you need to buy to do push-ups?

☛ ☛ ☛

Who was taking care of her kids when Marilyn Quayle was busy giving her speech about mothers staying at home?

☛ ☛ ☛

Why does television have 'seasons'? Is there a bad time to watch it?

☛ ☛ ☛

Has that guy who played Luke Skywalker ever worked again?

☛ ☛ ☛

Who is buying that Kathy Lee Gifford record and should we be worried about them?

☛ ☛ ☛

What kind of people buy cars because the commercial has a lot of good singing and dancing?

☛ ☛ ☛

If the Senate toilet is all male, who changes the toilet paper?

☛ ☛ ☛

What does it say about a car when the first thing they mention in their advertisements is the CD player?

☛ ☛ ☛

Can't we find a word for the difference between 'spicy' hot food and 'hot' hot food?

☛ ☛ ☛

The Ross Perot Paradox: If he's so rich, why isn't he smart?

☛ ☛ ☛

Why do they always name cars after things that will hurt you?

☛ ☛ ☛

What do you call a danish pastry in Denmark?

☛ ☛ ☛

Why does most exercise equipment end with the word *master*?

☛ ☛ ☛

If no man is an island, how come so many of them are atolls?

☛ ☛ ☛

Why can a thief charge things on my credit card when I can't?

☛ ☛ ☛

Why do people name their children Tiffany but not Bloomingdale's?

☛ ☛ ☛

Not all men are mechanically inclined. A friend tells me a story about the guy who went to the hardware shop and bought a chainsaw. The next day he brings it back.

'What's the matter?' says the clerk.

'You told me this saw would cut down ten trees in an hour. It took me all day yesterday to chop down ten trees.'

The clerk says, 'Let me look at it.' He takes the saw and pulls the starter cord. The thing starts right up with a deafening sound, a loud angry buzz. The customer puts his fingers in his ears and shouts to the clerk, 'What's making all that noise?'

☛ ☛ ☛

A lot of men are showing up at 'executive placement centres' now that the 80s are over. One woman got assigned to help a fiftyish guy get a new position. 'At my last job I was the chief financial officer of a big company and it was a great place to work. Their medical and dental plan covered me and my family. We got two months of sick leave. We got bonuses twice a year. They encouraged two-hour-long expense account lunches. I had a company car, a BMW.'

'So, why did you leave?' asked the woman.

'We went out of business.'

A woman was out in the park walking her dog. After a while she let him off the lead and made him perform a few tricks she had taught him.

A man who had been watching them walked over and asked her how she had taught the dog all those tricks. 'I can't get mine to roll over,' he said.

'It's easy to teach a dog,' said the woman. 'But first, you have to be smarter than the dog.'

☛ ☛ ☛

What's the quickest way to lose 180 pounds of ugly fat?

Divorce him.

☛ ☛ ☛

We sometimes wonder if there are any limits to a man's laziness.

I once heard two men talking.

One said, 'I'm thinking of going to Australia. The news says that someone's discovered a diamond mine in the outback where they sit all over the ground. All you have to do is bend down and pick them up.'

The other guy looked at his friend and said, 'Bend down?'

☛ ☛ ☛

I have often wondered if men are slobs naturally or if they learn it.

I remember one mother who had just had it with her young son who wouldn't clear up his room. When she couldn't stand it any more, she told him if he didn't clear it up, she would, and she'd charge him 50 pence for every item she picked up.

At the end of a week she grabbed him and said, 'You owe me six pounds, young man.'

He gave her a tenner and said, 'Thanks, Mum. Keep up the good work.'

Isn't it strange the way men think women think exactly like they do. They have an uncanny gift for spoiling a magic moment.

Once a man and a woman were making love but it wasn't working. Thinking he's saying exactly the right thing, the man looks at the woman and says, 'What's the matter? Couldn't you think of anybody, either?'

☛ ☛ ☛

What is the definition of an inconsiderate husband?

One who wins a trip for two to Paris and goes by himself twice.

☛ ☛ ☛

Whoever said marriage is a fifty-fifty proposition thinks five is half of one hundred.

☛ ☛ ☛

One day a six-year-old boy and his friends are looking at his family picture album.

When he gets to the parents' wedding portraits he nods in recognition, 'That's the day Mummy came to work for us.'

☛ ☛ ☛

They have something now called Marriage Anonymous. When you feel like getting married, you call somebody and they send over a man in a dirty T-shirt who hasn't shaved in three days, smells like beer, and watches football.